A Poet's Year

GEORGE MACBETH

A Poet's Year

LONDON
VICTOR GOLLANCZ
1973

ISBN 0 575 01742 2

ACKNOWLEDGEMENTS

Some of these poems have appeared, or will appear, in the following magazines: *Antaeus, Cosmopolitan, Encounter, The New Statesman,* and *The Times Literary Supplement.* One of them was a Sceptre Press pamphlet, one was commissioned by the Globe Playhouse Trust and published in *Poems for Shakespeare,* and one was commissioned by the Ilkley Literature Festival and printed in facsimile by The Scolar Press as part of the folio, *Tribute to Wystan Hugh Auden.*

CONTENTS

September
    The Stones   3
November
    The Vision   7
    The Pig Track   9
    To the Autumn   11
December
    On the Death of May Street   15
    A Farewell   16
January
    Towards Ulster   21
    Lighting an Oven   23
    Birth   25
    Listening to an Ambulance   27
    Bat   29
March
    Sarah's Room   33
April
    Lamps   37
    Lovers   40
    Afterwards   42
    Gloria's Letter   43
May
    The World of J. Edgar Hoover   47
June
    The Awakening   53
July
    Porn   57
    Postcards from Israel   59
    Flying Leaves   61
August
    Lovers Again   65
    A Life   67
September
    Time Passing   71

SEPTEMBER

THE STONES

If somewhere, high across
A distance of acute new stone,
  A line were drawn,
And followed fractures, as in a geode,
Along the war, it would lie over loss
  Everywhere. Each has his own,
As when, before these plots were watered lawn,
  I felt my house explode.

The stones remember. Each
In its filled grip of air retains
  A clot of scars,
And where, as here, a tower marks a square
Abandoned by the blast, I seem to reach
  Into a fuse, or towards a mains,
And feel, behind its windows, in their bars,
  Vibrating everywhere.

Darmstadt, 1971

NOVEMBER

THE VISION

for A. Young, d. 1971

It happens in an urn
   Whose glass mimes oak
Where acid made it burn.
I think I smell rough smoke.

It seems I lift my hand
   And rake edged leaves
From a grave. I understand
What shivers there, and heaves.

Lifted by art, its dream
   Broods to a cry.
In broken white, they stream,
Sick presences, that I

Scourge, but absorb. I read
   Their agony in
Its dark, amazing need.
It succours me, like skin.

I lack. Hail to that mast
   Where lie scoured lips,
Cold women, in their fast,
Soured from all lenten grips!

In salt they come, they freeze,
   Palled acorns: bled
Into the scope of knees,
Hands, and the groping head.

You knew it once. Old friend,
   Now wormed like stone,
I see you near the end
Writing in bed alone.

What can atone ? They come,
  The dead who keep
A little time, and a drum.
They lure me into sleep.

THE PIG TRACK

Yes, but the final detail
about the pig track,
how it was the quickest way,
starting above the hotel,
why do I leave that out?

I tell it as it was. The day
waned as we rose. Hour
after hour
seeped into the classic sea of Wales,
and my friends grew old.

This was a high occasion. Noble
in aspect and in
achievement. That five
such unexceptional and unathletic ones
should take the mountain

never seemed once amazing,
nor was then. We climbed at peace,
and in our own styles: Alaric
as always, bluff and sudden, Jock
like a sick dog,

Martin and I, together,
cool as a brace of dice
made out of ice, and
Xavier,
alas fat Xavier, as best he could.

We made it, as they say. Sat
for a talkative hour
on the peak, to see Caernarvon,
and came down. Of course,
there was lager first, and a wedge of cheese.

Draw down the blinds. It is
dark now. The light
settles, across the Estuary. Spick Alaric
is in his grave near Bodmin,
Jock has arthritis.

Never such elegance
to be commanded,
as ours was. We climbed the mountain,
Martin and Xavier,
those other two and I, five mortal friends.

> *Yes, but the final detail*
> *about the pig track,*
> *how it was the quickest way,*
> *starting above the hotel,*
> *why do I leave that out?*

10

TO THE AUTUMN

Through barren trees
Each Sunday, as this long November slows,
I age across the park. Where puddles freeze,
The oaks crust silver, and a sycamore snows

Leaves in the ride,
Though no tree feels the death-white mist and wind
As clammy as I do, through fleece and hide.
That clay-stiff wind ! I loathe it, and feel pinned

Into my pale
On the slopes of forty, though unreconciled
To a squirrel ageing, even to a snail.
The dank force masses, but the air is mild.

Somewhere, a breath
Of delicate festering, a sort of stew
Spirals, to taint the breeze. I breathe my death,
Dreaming of being born again, made new

By power and art,
And losing solid matter, like soiled clay
Off mouldering football-boots. I want to start
Fresh from the sloughings, free from all decay,

Light as a fly
In crisp October, when the final few
Shake out their wings, believing the rich dye
Will never fade, and brilliant in their blue.

At the door of birth
I pause, and count those left : the ones with tails
And iridescent glister, shot from earth
In Aztec richness, as their season ails.

11

They arc, and shine
Over the water, turquoise as they burn.
I am born with them, and make their fury mine,
Savaging the chill air. Silent, I turn

Where fire recedes
Across the river, as the sun declines.
I see the last one founder by the reeds.
Up from the mud, a grey dung-beetle whines.

DECEMBER

ON THE DEATH OF MAY STREET

for my grandfather

You built it, and baptised it with her name,
Sixty eight years ago. No angel came

That first Edwardian day to plant the stone
And make a child. Your wife conceived alone

And bore my mother in that soaking room
Where water later flowed, that choked her womb.

Tonight I write that May Street is condemned
And sure to die, as she was. Gripped and hemmed

By the sour blood of change, that rips and kills,
It dies far quicker than she did by pills.

I own it, and I see it broken, stone
By mother-naked stone. I heard her groan

That last night in our house before she died,
Not knowing how to help her. So I cried,

As I do now inside, to see her name
Shaken, and wasted. For your wasted fame

I cry to you, grandfather, in your grave
In rage and grief. All that you failed to save

Has shrunk to geometry, to crumbled lime
Beside the brickworks, to your grandson's rhyme.

A FAREWELL

I

Somewhere, I don't know where,
A nun with a glass eye

Touches a vase. Her blood
Runs into milk slowly.

Nowhere is there a man
Who knows why this is. So

I can write all I want
About it, knowing you.

II

Dara. Pam called today.
I see her often. If

You object write c/o
The Glass Company. Once

We made soup in a vase
Big enough to dress in.

Fairies on cabbages
Watched us. I know. You laugh.

III

Easy does it. First
We play a game of Cluedo.

As the bald Hispano-
Suiza turns into

Our drive, Maxim erects
A prestige hamburger.

All the starlets eat. One
Is sick on a tulip.

IV

Anyway. There was that
Nice time in South Molton,

Wasn't there? I begot
Image on image. You

Foxed every cadence.
Willy is now the rage

According to Elspeth.
Willy Yeats. That old shit.

V

Remember? In the grounds
Rocco was beating up

A servant. He used a
Jewelled swagger-stick. At

Six o'clock precisely
Your de Havilland *Moth*,

Dara, will land on the
Front lawn. So help me God.

VI

Don't ask why. Just step in.
I suppose the pilot

May be a woman. Left,
Then down the avenue.

I know. It rhymes. It all
Has to at times. At times

It seems best to believe
They do it for — what? For what?

VII

Final contrivings! Rust
On the bald limousine.

Fetch the *Kleenex*. Fast. And
Phone Rollo Lampeter.

Lust for fashion, they say,
Is all it is. And so

Nothing regrets nothing.
Acid eats the silver.

VIII

Poor Dara! You were lean
As a nip of cointreau

That last Friday. The wind
Ate your enamel hair.

Coughing, you set off. Down
Those grey allées, salutes

Of fans echoed. Look. The
De Havilland is here.

IX

Finally. To believe
In what is done, certain

It could not otherwise
Amount to more than a

Sport, frivolous delays
On the road to death, is

What gives one the title.
Farewell, Dara. God Bless.

New Year's Eve, 1971

JANUARY

TOWARDS ULSTER

Six feet of meat
Fried from the bath, I rise
   And dress to go.
Today the morning flies.
In a glass bowl, I flow
   Through broken sleet

Falling. With time,
I travel slow, and think,
   On a bad road.
Past forty, near the brink,
Violence is a code.
   I skid on slime

To the air. Pills
Taste sweet now, and I sit
   Far back, at ease.
A steward nips the slit
Of wind spirting. I freeze
   In height that kills.

Outside, night starts.
Cold, stepping down, I stare
   At a white can.
The savagery is bare.
Three soldiers, and a van,
   Clutch at the heart's

Too ready strings.
They meet me, and I drive
   By a bombed-out house.
Here, pity stays alive
Deep indoors, a cold mouse
   In a hole. Things

Cover their life
Oozing, tight, hot and strange
　Through fallen stones.
I sense, and taste, the range.
First, the road-humps, the cones
　Of civil strife

　That lifts, and fills.
A hard way back, I come
　To quench fire's weight
Of agony, like rum.
I sip the dust of hate
　From those charred sills.

　In a wide air
Above that ridden ground
　I hear the sun.
The engines make no sound.
I and a belted nun
　Eat steak, and stare.

LIGHTING AN OVEN

I see the wavering jets,
Lean, razor-blue blurs, rising from their holes
In blackened iron, as the fire begins
     And the air frets.
Over the small potatoes, humped in bowls
And scrubbed for baking in their earthen skins,
A steady wash of gradual violence rolls,

And stirs. How can their seeds,
Through molten juices, gather and return
Towards the ground, their mother, the far source ?
     Their virtue bleeds.
Embodied by their clothes, they lie and burn.
A hard soot stiffens to them, as the force
Intensities the lesson they must learn :

All changes balance change,
And, through the iron blades of ovens, heat
Emerges from thrown doors in tasty light
     Along the range
As food, as sustenance, as finished meat.
Are these potatoes, broken open, white
As naked children, balanced weights for sleet

I see descend like flame
Across my window, to the white, raw ground ?
Always it tastes of salt-rich blood, and stays,
     Untouched, the same.
Indoors, contained, unshaken by cold sound
Or by the pressured air that worms and slays,
These glands lie steady on a common mound.

They own a polished room,
Their hair cut short, their tubers shorn and scarred.
Their vulnerable surfaces subdued,
      I stroke their bloom
Under a glaze of salt. They seem baked hard
Into a perfect roughness, subtly rude.
Outdoors, a cat, undoctored, combs the yard

      For something he can strain
Into a privacy of boiling green
Where worms and grown potatoes sleep in soil.
      Dashed by the rain
Of sun-flecked air, he arcs in rusty sheen
On tabby black, like iridescent oil :
Such fetterless violence, entailed, obscene !

      Be still. Neither is right,
That human gathering, nor this natural drive.
I see the free cat, shag-worn in his mood,
      Who rolls in light
More lethal to the lilies than a knife
Along their plots. Unheeding, bloody-hued,
I dream of the potatoes, burned alive.

BIRTH

Swept by the sucked waste, out
Into a funnel of encrusted slime,
  Clutch to what hopes you can. In time,
Surviving to the mouth, crawl through the spout

  And live on white glaze, black
As any target to the eye of death
  In cat or man. For drawing breath
It has to be the dark folds you most lack.

  So live and win. Displayed
Along enamel, with a severed leg
  A foot away, eat up your egg,
I mean your fear, and grow towards the shade.

  Something will happen. Slow,
Tired by the light, slur over the smooth ground,
  And reach the opening. You found
It easier before, thrown by the flood?

  I know. Lower yourself
Through what looks brass, and solid. Years before,
  It seems, you fought here, blind and sore.
Feel for the ridges, for the first rough shelf.

  It takes your weight. So rest.
There is a time for waiting, as for work,
  Even in this coarse tube of mirk.
So drop at ease, grown ready for each test

  In dint of progress. One
Bruised inch of stench, then one again:
  Soft body to the round wall. Then
Swung over the abyss, the silk rope's run

Holding you taut. From your
Own body, as that sticky length extends,
   The future is explored, and bends.
Go easy, if at all, through its black sewer.

   Up from the ground, a light,
As if from too far off to matter, seeps :
   Bald darkness in the middle creeps
And alters, from each end, the drip of white.

   So move more fast. I hear,
Or think I do, the turning of a tap.
   Be still. The plug is in. No slap
Of iron on you yet, no cause for fear

   Until the chain runs. Then,
Lie loose, and dive. There has to be a chance.
   Buried in water, like a lance,
You may survive the battering of men,

   You may be flung safe, clear
Of the enamel gutter, from the waste.
   Be fortunate, if so. Make haste
And roll to where some darker hand can steer

   A better luck. There grow
Another leg. There bless the world, and eat.
   I send you now. It comes, more fleet,
More terrible, more cold than long ago,

   The flood of birth. Sink in
From what the pipe once offered, a safe nest.
   The time is past for birth, and rest.
The flood of death is starting to begin.

26

LISTENING TO AN AMBULANCE

Torn from my sleep
By a klaxon revving, I begin my run.
The world screams. In a bloody heap,

Holding a gun,
I seem to rise from bed-clothes, dazed and red,
Into the day, the flying sun.

I pile my dead
Along the chest-of-drawers. Aware and green
With what is growing in my head,

I take the clean,
The human, the unwounded, naked light
Into my mind, and make it mean.

The horn bleeds white,
Aborting sound along the rain. Again,
It seems to hiss, deliberate, slight.

Slack sounds of pain !
A siren, or a fire-bell, I can bear :
Not this black, searing under-stain

Out of bare air
And skinning me. They visit all in time.
So let them sacrifice, or spare :

Not stir the slime
Where ordinary, mudful spawn can wake
And croak away, before the lime.

27

c

It comes. All break,
Fail, soon enough, without that haunting wail
To pin them to a bloody stake.

I rise. Grown stale
With avarice and dreams, I shave, and deep
Inside my brain, worn circuits fail.

BAT

Voided. Not lost. Ago
Was when it happened, edge of tooth on moss
    Despoiled in red,
Now anxious for the bits, fragmented floss
To come back. At a finial's, winter's, toe,
    Light fled,

Was genital. Eye-beads
Glazed, am a poor, drawn shadow now. Black noise
    Rattles like snow
On torn slate flakes. What answers out of poise
Is as reflectors bleating. It all needs
    To slow,

Be lifted, screened in time.
Begin to come. A lady's little scent
    Eats at my ears
In an elastic yawn. Closed in a tent
Of viscous green, one enveloped in slime
    Grows, nears

And is born, shorn of light
As fibres tear. Flaps, floating, mark of hair
    Across a sky
Bloated with fallen leaves. Turns you two bare,
Closed, in a walk. I hear, beyond all flight,
    Far cry

From violence-induced
Urgency of the ground. There grown, things grate
    Against raw skin,
Crawl through, drawn to a future, and inflate,
Or stiffen. One will crow, ghost on a roost,
    Hair-thin.

MARCH

SARAH'S ROOM

Proust got rushes when his rats were
Punctured with a pin

The door is clinking on the latch,
  And no-one now is in :
The kitchen stirs. And Sarah's room
  Shivers like my skin.

Sarah is out, and I am here,
  Alone upon her mat.
I lie and write a loving note,
  With drawings of a cat.

The logs are sinking on her hearth,
  It's growing rather late.
The pictures that I gave her burn
  Against the blackened slate.

I remember, I remember,
  A dog that ran away.
Sarah's head was in my hand,
  And Rover's hair was grey.

Stop the picture, close the flies,
  I can hear a car.
The Wonder Book of Reptiles wants me,
  And the door's ajar.

I mean I knew, I mean I knew,
  It was quite a thing
Polishing a bit of rubber
  To make a wedding ring.

The door is clinking on the latch,
   And someone else is in.
I am in the garden, and
   Sarah's in the bin.

Proust got rushes when his rats were
Punctured with a pin

APRIL

LAMPS

I

as if
burning
  seeds of

a pomegranate
  in
cabriole ivory, you

  exude
thunderstorms of
  immaculate plastic

II

  lascivious
root, omerging
  fatigued

  through
tight, lacy
  knickers of

  seven
iridescent
  nipples

III

  dragon's
pierced orifice
  on

a bracket,
  hinged
for a massacre

37

amidst
degenerate
  toadstools

IV

reflections of
tulips, blur
  through smoke,

  as if
"designed for a Cleveland man"
  meant

  only fluting, a
crinkle edge
  to cigars

V

Russian
lemons, dipped
  from

  a fluorescent
balloon of
  wasp-waisted

  elastic, as
delicate as a monkey's
  testicles

VI

  metallic
wedding-cake, a
  ticklish

howdah
submerging
a single

enormous
acorn's
incandescence

VII

as a spider
clawing
over a ceiling

hooked
with obstreperous
tiles,

bloat.
raw, and uneasy,
you steal

LOVERS

One night we ate, and then lay down
    Under a slab of stone.
The Green was dark, and dog-shit stank
    Against my ankle-bone.

That happened later. At the time
    I noticed only fox,
Smell of her coat along the ground,
    And pressure of a box.

The wind was cold. We lay and screwed,
    As happy as we could.
I mean, you're better off out there
    Than wormed-through under wood.

So we got home. Unsatisfied,
    She lay and watched the stars.
Far off, a hundred yards away,
    I heard the passing cars.

We cleaned my shoe with soap. It stank
    For days on end of shit.
So did her kitchen. As she said,
    You're never shot of it.

It's true. Last night, I dreamed of her,
    Jealous, and vaguely lost.
I woke, and took a parcel in,
    And wondered what it cost.

The sense of death, the sense of loss,
    A sort of worried guilt.
Yes, it was worth it, as we were,
    Better than with a quilt

Hours later. So we had it off
   Amidst the corpses there.
Her skirt was up above her thighs,
   Four inches of them bare.

That, and the dog-shit, I recall,
   And will in later years.
Broken lady, flaunt your columns,
   Virginity is tears.

AFTERWARDS

I

Normal life resumed. It was organised, lovely, and bland,
And so I hid the revolver in the darkness of my hand.

II

Somewhere, I heard men singing. The moon was pinned
　　to a wall.
An echo became a crystal, and a rifle shrank to a shawl.

III

There was nothing to feel except pity, anguish along the
　　groin,
Ice on a station window, and a woman's head on a coin.

IV

Virility, activate silence. It never succeeds like success,
The leading-edge of a razor, or the menstrual blood on a
　　dress.

V

King Billy, Cromwell. Name them, as they come.
The world sinks to the muffled thud of a drumstick on a
　　drum.

GLORIA'S LETTER

I

Dear John, I thought you'd like to know,
    I'll kill you, if I can,
Unless you leave your childish wife,
    And learn to be a man.

It's getting more than I can bear
    To live alone up here
In Hampstead, and I want you back,
    As soon as may be, dear.

II

Well, well, I thought, that's rather bad,
    I'd better lock the door.
But still, she'll come and scream outside,
    And call my wife a whore.

The telephone's still on the hook,
    And soon we'll hear it ring.
A woman scorned feels pretty tough,
    And Gloria's mind's like string.

It ties you up in cutting knots
    Until your sinews burn.
You can't get loose however much
    You try to twist and turn.

So drive to her, says I to me,
    As naked as a pear.
It won't do any good, you know,
    To kiss her lovely hair.

43

D

So take her nipples in your hands
   With all the skill you've got,
And that, from what the papers say,
   Is really quite a lot.

III

Dear John, it wouldn't do, my boy,
   I'm not so daft as that.
I've bought some liquor for my friend,
   And locked us in my flat.

If you come there, the police will come,
   And throw you into jail,
Frustrated as a leper with
   A can tied to your tail.

So go away, or come away,
   Be mine, or never mine,
You bloody, stupid, little, fucking,
   Meretricious swine !

MAY

THE WORLD OF J. EDGAR HOOVER

There wasn't time to take a gun, and follow through the
    turns.
Nothing to do but hammer back, with a halo and your
    burns.

I go into Chicago, and I go into Yale,
And they take my face with a proper grace, and a plate
    of rice and kale.

Somebody was clever, and somebody was true,
Their hats were down on their hard eyes, and they died
    to make me glue.

Talk to Alexander, and talk to Hitler, too,
They weren't the same as I was, with their heads and
    their men in blue.

If anything could matter, it wasn't where you were
The night they caught Capone, and tossed him in the
    stir.

Black eyes, blue eyes, it's all the same in hell
When they ring the bloody changes, and you crack the
    passing-bell.

I took out my revolver, and I took it out to kill,
With a death's-head on my harness, and a tranquillising
    pill.

I cried for my machine-gun, I cried to make them come,
The women with the honey, and the men who turned
    their thumb.

So try a little harder, and keep your money shut,
The world slows to stardom, and all police-work's for a
  slut.

America, I loved you, I hung you on my wall,
As anxious and exotic as a show-girl at a ball.

Now it's nearly over, I lie and scream in bed
For a handful of your hard nuts, and some silence in my
  head.

I hear the fires frying, and the cannon in my brain,
And the past seems to gush and spirt, like rubbish down
  a drain.

"Listen, Mr. Hoover, I need a place to go" –
O.K., so make it Sing-Sing, and take your ten years slow.

I broke him for his arrogance, he took a money rap,
And another with his brother, like a ferret in a trap.

I get explicit dying, I can hear the choppers clack,
Or are they red-neck ravens, with a warrant on their
  back?

Into ice and shadow, into night I come,
With an ice-chip on my shoulder, and a last glass of rum.

"Listen, Mr. Hoover, it's 1972,
And the skids are on the century, and all you tried to do.

So it's out with Al Capone, and it's out with Dillinger,
And as for Mistress Bonny, why, you've had your lot of
  her."

Well, let them scream and settle, the vultures on my time,
I never heard of any state that never heard of crime.

48

I took it by its rough throat, I shook it into life,
And for fifty years it came to bed, and I screwed it like a
    wife.

So lie and love your little men, your Johnsons and
    your Jews,
I'm not afraid of how it sounds when you read it in the
    news.

I was the man who pushed them, I held their sweating
    hands,
And I cleaned their bottoms for them, at the hokey-
    pokey stands.

"Into Guatemala now, or anywhere at all,
Into Cuba, into Vietnam," hear the bugles call

Just like Kipling for the limeys, beautiful and clear:
All they saw was theirs to have, and they broke it like a
    steer.

"Yes, but we had our reasons, we had to do what's
    right" —
And I was there to clear the mess, and sweep the shit
    from sight.

I was the cause and action, I watched with a cold eye
Their life and death, as Yeats did, like a cadillac pass by.

Heaped with flowers, and letters, your century goes
    down,
As masterful as Nineveh, and as cruel as a clown.

The wheels are turning slowly, and the mafia slope arms,
Before your Irish wolf-hounds, with their red hair and
    their charms.

The hearse is made of walnut, and the mounts are brass
and gold,
And underneath the lot I lie, like an egg kept warm in
mould,

The conscience of your blood-lust, and the broomstick
of your will,
As useless to the future as a government by skill.

Tomorrow to Belfast I ride, and tomorrow to Japan,
With a Thomson gun, or an atom bomb, and a throw of
sand in a pan.

It never ends, the violence It drives, and always will.
So take your time, and think it out, and remember who
must kill.

The professionals, like I was, know. We take it in our
stride,
And what we can't dispose of quick, we learn the way
to hide.

Good-night, America. And drop me in the ground.
Let the earth fall across my chest, like the muzzle of a
hound.

JUNE

THE AWAKENING

I

On the first screen, a hawk
Squats on the branch of a

Plum-tree, which is covered
With snow, and blossoming :

*Out of decay there shall come
Initiative, and slow unfolding.*

II

On the second screen, five
Stallions are in their stalls, over

Which a beautiful tree,
Perhaps a willow, droops

Edged leaves. A mare is at
The end of the line, in her stall :

*Never believe in loneliness, the
World is white with love.*

III

On the third screen, a rack
Of good lacquer is carrying

A kimono, and other garments.
One is patterned, most

Exquisitely, in my opinion,
With about seven fans :

*Trust in the surfaces, they
Will reveal a hanging glory.*

IV

On the fourth screen, a remarkable
Red-breasted bird is on

A rock, beside a stream
Where others, more easy to

Identify, are walking, or
Flying. There is also a waterfall:

*Take the colour for what
It is, be amazed by nothing.*

V

On the fifth screen, which is
The first of a pair, a bridge

Crosses a grooved river, beside
A water-wheel. Each rim

Of the wheel is the *mon*
Of the Doi:

*Even the most ordinary detail
Can be a surprising wonder.*

VI

On the sixth screen, which is
The second of the same pair, the moon

Dips above another bridge
And a willow scatters petals:

*All is gold, and a sort
Of bronze gleam on the gold.*

JULY

PORN

I

on the sofa
nurse's dress
  bra under it
fondled them
  sucked at my
caressing

II

preparing Sunday
closed over my
  fondling me
astride
  minus panties

III

menstruating
one more
  brushing my
up my night-dress
  tantalising him by

IV

in our underwear
steady trickle
  round my
emptied herself

V

pulled up her
in peach silk, *directoire*
  on her knees and legs
tucking it
  took me through a

VI

bent over
"Please Yes." he gasped
and I felt his
under my
moving higher
pressure of
erupted

POSTCARDS FROM ISRAEL

I

Jerusalem

In the American Colony, you can type.
Olives for lunch. It's happening. There's a Pole

With a number on his arm. In a glut of tripe-
sludge undersea, you feel nightmares unroll.

II

Eilat

Imagine ! All those Jews denying fish
On a Friday. Thirteen crowns, like thistle-heads

Being cast down, as if to make a wish
In a well. Sea urchins angle in their beds.

III

Ein-Gedi

The *Minox* clickings ! Lazy eyes, and lips
Munching. Triangular cough-sweets. How the soul

Sweats from its toil ! Bodies stink worse than chips.
Remember ? The Dead Sea was Joshua's bowl.

59

E

IV

Acre

Wherever you are, there's an Armenian joke
About the *droit de seigneur*. I eat meat.

The priest has my woman, while I choke.
Nothing but snapper's flesh, white, thick, and sweet.

V

Tel Aviv

So it ends. I'll be back shortly, via Rome
In an air-taxi. To be stricken, free

From the vice of Hebrew love, clamp of the dome !
Praise to the dream, the ungovernable sea !

FLYING LEAVES

I

The tremendous thunder-claps
of God's uneven fences !

Disc jockeys
relieve themselves in my arm-pits,

or so it seems,
when I listen to *Wozzeck*

on my ear-trumpet.
You have to believe me

when I tell you it really
happened.

II

Eloquently,
the rain patters onto

the last scute
of chrysanthemums. And Millicent

is still pouring
green tea

on my samisen.
Decorum for Christmas.

III

That's what *I* want.
An egg with a taste

of normal people. No more
American hens

with their bloody suicides
in the small hours.

IV

Or, for that matter,
the "rage to live",

stifling initiative
with soda-water.

V

Be a great composer.
Yes. But never on Sundays,

David,
or before the children.

AUGUST

LOVERS AGAIN

That day we started
By the sea.
With a woman's buttocks
On your knee,

It isn't easy
To move hard.
Nevertheless,
I did. And, starred

With the lights of Boscombe
In her eyes,
She tried my probing
Cock for size.

You don't like language
Bare like this,
Do you? You'd
Prefer a kiss.

OK, we kissed,
Her tongue along
My foreskin :
And she sucked me strong

Until we came
(Later)
Together. But not then.
I couldn't sate her

With couples walking
Hand in hand,
And an orange sail-boat
On the sand

In darkness. Later,
On my floor,
White carpet stretched
That made her sore,

I brought her back
To the sound of surf,
Shingle rolling,
And green turf,

Airs of night,
And my bloody sons.
Aren't such dreams
Everyone's ?

A LIFE

after Hokusai

I

The blinds come down. The candle dies,
And universal darkness lies

All round the world. I have the wife.
I smoke a pipe. It makes a life.

II

I smoke a pipe. And, in my dream,
Enjoy a mushroom soup, with cream.

There's bread and buttor, too. And first,
A glass of beer, to quench my thirst.

It's English food-time. Free for all,
A plate of soup, and a meat-ball

With Heinz tomato ketchup. Meat
For everyone, tasty and sweet,

A baked potato, swedes and beans,
And some new carrots. But no greens.

Dessert then. Ice-cream, or a cake:
Madeira, fairy, chocolate-flake,

Or devil's-food. Then coffee (white)
A nip of *Teacher's*, and good-night.

III

The blinds come down. The candle dies,
And universal darkness lies

All round the world. I have the wife.
I smoke a pipe. It makes a life.

SEPTEMBER

TIME PASSING

I

And did they run
Together down
Towards the sea ? And was it dark ?
And who was there ?

Was anyone
Besides the two
Sisters ? Was Aubrey there ? And was
It really cold ?

II

And was the tide
Receding, with
An undertow ? And did they care ?
And did the girls

Change on the sands,
Or beforehand
In the caravan ? And did the moon
Come out and show

Then shivering
Between the groynes,
Their bodies whetted, rubbed with salt,
And bare as knives

Mounting the water as
The kings and queens
On playing-cards ? And did they laugh
And fall in waves ?

71

III

And did their hands
Or icy hips
Touch underwater, and withdraw?
And did the surge

Pull down their hearts
To its own cold?
And did the night
Seem long and full

With empty riches,
And the world
Float in their eyes
For a great distance?

IV

Yes. It did.
And did the watch
One dropped as he
Came wading in

Jam, with the time
For ever in
Its glassy face? And is it there
Imperishable in

The green, a joy
And care to come
For all of them? And will they know
Before they die?

V

No. They will not.
And as they dry
Their sanded flesh
And walk away, a bitter wind

Whitens the breath
Each gives to air.
And do they know?
No. They do not. And never will.

September 1st, 1972